Who's Your Copilot?

How to Get the Most from Your Business Coaching Engagement

Dru Babcock

Speaker – Peak Performance Coach – Pilot

PowerCurveCoaching.com

For permission requests, contact the publisher at

Stearns Media Group
5982 Harcourt Drive
Coeur d'Alene, ID 83815

Power Curve Coaching
2269 Chestnut St # 247
San Francisco, CA 94123-2600

First edition.
Printed in the United States of America

$14.95USA
Business/Leadership

Babcock, Dru
Who's Your Copilot? An Entrepreneur's Guide to Getting the Most from a Business Coaching Engagement/ Dru Babcock.—1st ed.

Published by Stearns Media Group

Cover Design: Carl Stearns

ISBN-13: 978-1507884867
ISBN-10: 1507884869

DEDICATION

To my life partner, wife and mother of my children Andrea Babcock, and my daughter Sloan Babcock, as well as my dear parents Jim, Carol and Michelle, and all my sisters, brothers and cousins. Thank you for your beautiful souls, support and constant inspiration! Serving you is the central purpose in my life.

TABLE OF CONTENTS

ACKNOWLEDGMENTS

My world-class Team of trainers and coaches at RRI: Marc, Jayne, Brenda, Mike, Ben, Debra, Dave, Tony, Mary as well as all of my many, many coaching and flight clients whom I have made incredible distinctions with. And my flight mentors Kathy and Tom. Also Erik and Debi. A big thank you to Joe and Alison Williams for assisting me with my public presence and seminars. And thank you to all of my critics, nay-sayers and worthy opponents throughout my lifetime who helped me to focus on being my absolute best self so that I could overcome adversity and be on the path to mastery.

> Nothing is particularly hard if
> you divide it into small jobs
>
> Henry Ford

INTRODUCTION

Coaching has been a part of our societal fabric for thousands of years. People instinctively know that behind every great athlete and every athletic team is a coach. It goes without saying.

When it comes to business; however, we tend to expect that we have to go it alone. That success in our careers, businesses and lives should be sole products of our actions. This simply is not true.

Since you are reading this book, I can safely assume that you no longer believe this to be the case and that you are considering whether or not a business coach might be a good option for you.

I wrote this book to provide entrepreneurs, just like you, a simple and concise guide to the selection and use of a business coach. It is my conviction that successful entrepreneurs deserve effective coaching. Just as great athletes deserve great coaches. In my experience, an epic client-coach relationship is the result of good chemistry, preparation, and commitment on both sides of the relationship.

I divided this brief book into eight sections with several exercises and videos. It is easy to follow along, and I invite you to contact me with your questions and comments.

> People are not lazy. They simply have
> impotent goals - that is, goals that do
> not inspire them.
>
> Tony Robbins

CHAPTER 1

THE CONCEPT OF

BUSINESS COACHING

If you currently or have ever played any sport you know how valuable it can be to your development to have a coach. A coach can see your form, pick up on things you can't see in yourself and apply what he or she has learned from working with other players. There's no doubt, in the world of sports; coaches are invaluable. Apply this same concept to your business or life for that matter.

Like coaches in sports, business coaches and life coaches' work with everyday people coaching them through business decisions and life's hurdles giving an outside perspective and the motivation to move forward and break down barriers.

I am a private pilot, flight instructor, a FAA certified Airline Transport Pilot and have worked as a commercial pilot. Moving up through my aviation career exposed me to several "coaching" relationships.

The first was during my flight instruction. As a new pilot, I had the passion and drive to become a pilot but I lacked the real world experience to do so. I had to learn every detail of flight; not only takeoff and landing but also mindset in the face of emergencies. This coaching relationship was more the master passing on his experience and observation to me so that I could develop my skills and knowledge.

Later in my aviation career I became a commercial pilot. Again I was in an instructor type "coaching" relationship but not in the same way as my initial flight training. Now I had the knowledge, experience and mindset to fly an airplane. My instructor was now tasked with taking me, a professional pilot, and helping me to develop the additional skill necessary to move to the next type of aircraft and the specialized procedures required. He was helping me grow in my career.

Then as a commercial pilot in command I entered into a new type of coaching relationship with my co-pilot. Not one where my "coach" was more experienced than I or a relationship where his job was to instruct me, but more of a mutual relationship that allowed me to do my job better. My co-pilot made me a better, safer, and more successful pilot in command. He provided me with an extra set of eyes, a resource to help in emergencies and someone who could recognize something I might have missed or might not have had the opportunity to notice. My co-pilot provided a partnership that helped grow my career and do my job better.

The question is; what type of coach do you need?

Most people reading this book are probably not newbie business people with no business experience or knowledge. I don't think an instructor relationship would be the right choice for you. However, a partner type "co-pilot" coaching relationship would be appropriate to your situation. A "co-pilot" coach that could help you take your business and career life to the next level. A "co-pilot" that can provide the necessary resources, insight, and navigation to help you do your job and live your life the way you want; bigger and better.

In most cases, people consider either going with a business coach or a life coach. Both of which provide valuable resources in their specific areas of expertise, which can help you make the most of the things you are doing in life. Here is a look at the similarities and differences between a life coach and a business coach, such as myself, in order to help you determine which may be best for you.

A life coach is someone who provides insight on how to manage your time, on what you should be focusing, and also help you continue to stay motivated in times when you feel like you aren't making progress. A life coaches' insight is directed to your professional life and career. Many also address everyday life decisions such as relationships and your profession.

A business coach, such as myself, is not a business consultant or personal therapist. As a business coach my job is to develop a trusted partnership with you in the success of your business. I am there to help you diagnose issues within your business so you can address those issues and move forward to even greater success.

Unlike a consultant, as a business coach, I am not there to jump in to take care of your problems for you. In fact, in most cases, I wouldn't have nearly the industry specific experience that you have to do just that. My job is to be there for straight to the point discussions, to provide an outsiders perspective that you can consider and keep you accountable to your tasks so you can achieve your business goals.

It's important to remember that there should be a balance in your life between personal and professional aspirations. Therefore, a life coach and a business coach both provide input into your life that can help you strive to reach the things you desire. If you want, consider bringing both into your life and meet with each individually to help you maximize your efforts. Or, if you feel like you are simply lacking in one area and could use some guidance, you can find a coach that fits that specific need.

> The highest destiny of the individual
> is to serve rather than rule.
>
> Albert Einstein

CHAPTER 2

THE ROLE OF A

BUSINESS COACH

Thinking of a business coach in terms of a co-pilot greatly simplifies your understanding of a business coaches' role in your life. It is not the job of a business coach to take over your business or project for you. Just like it is not the job a co-pilot to do the job of the captain. Though in some cases a business coach, like a co-pilot, often possess the skills to do your job, that is not the role of a business coach.

A business coach is there to help you recognize what it will take to get you to your peak performance. They do this by helping you define your goals and help you to develop your skills to enable you to reach those goals.

Like a co-pilot, a business coach does not necessarily have to possess the skill level, knowledge or experience you may have in your field of business to help you achieve your goals. This is where many people get confused between a business coach and a business consultant.

A business consultant often has a high level of hands-on expertise in a specific field and provides direct advice or steps in to help you with a specific aspect of your business or project. This often requires advanced skill levels and business experience directly related to your field.

A business coach, on the other hand, is there to help provoke thought and creativity to enable you to maximize your personal potential. Coaches' help you understand who you are, where you want to go and develop the strategies with you that you need to get you there.

Despite, not being an expert in every facet of a business, it is important to remember that a business coach is most valuable in one important area: seeing the big pictures.

Specifically, these might include:

- How can I better balance my business and personal life?
- How can I develop my business skills as well as my intellectual abilities?
- What are my business and personal strengths and weaknesses?
- Are their business opportunities that I

might not be taking full advantage?

- Are there other business professionals and organizations that might help me grow that I am not aware?

- How can I grow my business despite what might be considered transitional times?

- How can I develop plans to improve areas of my business and professional life that might be lacking, and I can improve?

In addition to all of the areas above, another important function--perhaps the most important function--of a business coach is to help inspire and motivate you to the successful accomplishment of your goals and ideals.

What Should You Expect From a Business Coach?

Here are a few things to think about when determining how a business coach could impact your life:

Insight

A business coach should always give you something to think about. Often these things will be difficult for you to address, and many require some soul searching. This insight might not always be welcome at first but having someone that can get you to think deeper about your challenges, and opportunities will enable you to grow rather than stagnate.

Fresh Perspective

Problems are opportunities to grow and sometimes it's hard to see that opportunity when you're the one suffering from the problem. A business coach provides an unhindered perspective that should help you discover new ways to solve your problems or at the very least see the glimpse of light that is just around the next cycle.

Inspiration

A business coach should cause you to want to act on the insights that you develop for the betterment of your business and life.

Motivation

Your work with a business coach should excite you and motivate you to move to the next level in your life and business.

Firm

Though a business coach can certainly be a friend. She shouldn't be beholden to you. She should give you straightforward observations and hold you accountable.

Mutual Respect

Do you respect each other, your educations,

knowledge, professionalism, and much more? If you don't respect each other, you can't learn from each other either.

Trust

It is important that from the beginning that you both trust each other. If you don't trust each other, you won't feel comfortable sharing information that is critical to the success of your business.

Partnership

You and your business coach are there to build a better business through a partnership. Your business coach is your copilot, not your instructor.

Expectations

Your business coach will help you develop realistic expectations that take you out of your comfort level and help you grow your business.

> All of our dreams can come true -if we
> have the courage to pursue them.
>
> Walt Disney

CHAPTER 3

BENEFITS OF A BUSINESS COACH

Some of the most successful businesses and personalities in different fields owe part of their might to having a professional coach. There are various benefits and reasons for working with a coach although not all those who hire such services are successful at realizing the claimed benefits. Besides, there is only so much that a coach can add, and a great deal is expected of the individual or business. However, the big question often remains how to work effectively with a business coach and succeed.

Here is a detailed discussion that includes tips, insights and ways of collaborating with professional coaches to achieve set targets:

The Johari Window

The Johari window created in 1955 by psychologists, Joseph Luft, and Harrington Ingham. I use it in my coaching practice to help my clients better understand their relationships, themselves, as well as how they relate to the people they lead in their business.

The Johari Window has four spaces that have different implications. The diagram is simply illustrated as benefits of knowing oneself, and letting another person know you. Its four spaces are briefly described as follows:

- **Open Arena** – This is the main quadrant in

	Known by Self	Unknown by Self
Known by Others	OPEN ARENA	BLIND SPOT
Unknown by Others	MASK	POTENTIAL

the diagram and represents that part of you which you are well aware of and so is the coach. In a business context, the quadrant represents issues of market equity, reputation, public image, staff capacity and efficiency among other observable elements.

- **Blind Spot** – This is the quadrant your coach sees in you but of which you have no concept. The blind spot is usually where a coach influences most although they also have heavy duties for the arena. Working with a coach enables your business to gain those special and unique insights and knowledge.

- **Mask** – This quadrant represents that area that you are aware of, but the coach is unaware. Masks are associated with negative energies and fear imposed reservations that may limit your potential to expand and develop. It is important to eliminate as many masks as possible moving those issues into the Arena where coaches can assist.

- **Potential** – This is perhaps the most interesting quadrant in Johari Window. It represents those elements of you that neither you nor your coach are aware. It seeks to identify one's true potential and facilitate reaching such targets.

The Johari window is only one coaching model that is put to practice for businesses. There are many other methodologies laid out depending on the individual nature of a business. For one to successfully work with a coach, they need to understand various things about the nature of their relationship and what each side is bringing into the business.

Nature of coach relationships

It is important for individuals and businesses to acknowledge their prime influence on matters regarding their operations and goals. A coach is an accountability partner who also bears witness to progress. Coaches will offer professional insight, motivation, administered training, preparation tests, monitoring techniques and ways of measuring performance. Coaching is often about identifying current position, goals, targets and the creation of a plan that when effectively executed will meet these.

A coach's duty is to accelerate progress rather than initiate it. Before contracting coaching services, the business person or business leadership must have already identified why it needs a coach in the first place, and this means there already exist targets. Coaches are supposed to offer ways of attaining more progress with less effort and within a shorter period. With the assistance of the coach, achieving targets should be easier, less painful and more preferably pleasurable to an extent.

Things to note

When working with a coach, nothing should be hidden since these are the aspects for which a coach is hired. There are a few things to take note of in order to succeed with the help of a business coach. Some of them include the following;

Communication –

Communication is perhaps a general concept most people and businesses are aware. However, it is surprising how many are still struggling with issues of effective communication with their coaches. The type of communication in question entails clear illustration of plans; research completed, designs proposed and processes in place for daily implementation. In short, the coach should elaborate all the plans and processes before the commencement to make sure your business is ready for implementation and appropriate modifications.

Control, Tracking, and Evaluation –

At the end of the day, coaches are supposed to induce positive progress that then ties them to evaluation. All controls put in place should allow for assessment of their effectiveness. There should be clear understanding of how outcomes are to be measured and interpreted. Control and measurement of outcomes should not be put off until the end of the coaching period. Rather, there should be periodical evaluations possible to achieve and use in tracking progress.

Responsibilities –

Issues of resource coordination, meeting schedules and responsibilities must be discussed prior to engagement. As an accountability partner, coaches will rarely indulge in motivation and building determination. It is upon the individuals to make sure they are available in due time for implementation of strategies, learning and practice so that decisions are made based on informed context of the situation.

There are other considerations to note

including coaching fees, materials, contingency plans and costs of taking part in the coaching activity. It's often wise to go through the profiles of a couple of coaches before hiring them to ensure you have a clear understanding of the nature of their work.

Working with business coaches has been known to yield tremendous results with the use of least effort in a more relaxed and comfortable fashion that depicts optimum efficiency. However, not all coaches will perform, and only a few succeed. A lot is upon the business owners who must have a clear distinction between their responsibilities and goals and those of the coach. Nonetheless, with the right models applied, coaching can be a great opportunity for business leaders and the people they lead.

In any moment of decision, the best
thing you can do is the right thing, the next
best thing is the wrong thing, and the
worst thing you can do is nothing.

Theodore Roosevelt

CHAPTER 4

HOW BUSINESS COACHING

WORKS

In business coaching you are the Captain; your employees are the team, and your business coach is your "co-pilot." As the Captain, it is your job to bring your business expertise, your dreams, and your agenda. As "co-pilot" it is the responsibility of the business coach to help you use your business skills to identify and realize your goals.

Business coaching is often delivered in the following two formats or a hybrid of both.

- One-on-One Coaching, and
- Group Coaching

Each of these session formats can be in person or through the use of telephone or internet streaming services. Your comfort, schedule, location, and goals would help determine the type of session appropriate to you. In this chapter, I will discuss the benefits and opportunities of each so that you can determine what will work best for you.

One-on-one

One-on-one is the most common form of business coaching; especially with executive members and business owners. A primary reason for this is not only the confidentiality it provides but the ability to focus on specific individualized needs.

One-on-one business coaching is usually conducted on a weekly or monthly basis with each session lasting about 30 minutes. Most sessions will start with the client reporting on the results of the last session's action items and perhaps some issues they'd like to explore further. It is a good idea to have a clear understanding of what you want out of each session prior to your scheduled time. This gives you the best opportunity to get the most of out the session.

Here are some of the pros and cons of participating in One-on-one business coaching.

Pros:
- Promotes operational communication and feedback.

- Provides opportunities for out-of-the-box leadership training.
- Creates an operational partnership.
- Creates the atmosphere of trust, confidentiality, and constant improvement.
- Emphasizes development for the future
- Supports operational performance management and productivity.
- Provides a vehicle for personal accountability.
- Allows the coach to provide a sometimes blunt perspective of the client's situation without embarrassment.

Cons

- Requires a measure of self-discipline to be effective. (No peer pressure)
- Often more challenging for individuals than in group sessions. One-on-one requires active participation rather than

passive listening.

- Fees will be higher than in group coaching; but so should outcomes.

Group Coaching

In group coaching, you will participate in the coaching session with other people who have a similar set of requirements. These groups may have as little as three participants and up to 30 participants that typically meet on a weekly or monthly basis. Group sessions are great for managers and employees in the same company or executives and business owners from separate non-competing companies.

Here are some of the pros and cons of the group coaching format.

Pros

- You choose your level of participation. You can actively participate or passively learn from others by listening.

- Learn from others – It is common in group sessions for the others to have experienced common issues and offer ideas that you might not have considered without this group perspective.

- You get support from more than one person. During one-on-one coaching sessions, you only get backing from one person - your coach.

- You will feel "less odd". In a coaching group, you will discover that other people have related challenges, weaknesses, visions and goals as you. Your difficulties will suddenly look a lot smaller than they did to you beforehand.

- Group sessions build confidence by letting you actively participate in helping others overcome challenges that you have faced.

- Sometimes, when appropriate, group

sessions are recorded allowing you to review the sessions again at a later time.

- Group coaching is often less expensive than one-on-one coaching. However, many people participate in both.

Cons

- Doesn't offer the opportunity to focus on individual requirements.
- You may have to be tolerant and wait if you want to bring up a subject that is different from what everyone else wishes to discuss.
- Offers less confidential; especially when group sessions involve employees from the same company.
- Though group sessions do increase accountability, it is often easy to dodge that accountability.

Goal setting

First entrepreneurs should be doing with their coach, is to set goals. If your coaching program lasts for 2-6 months, you'll want to set up short and long terms goals. It's essential to ensure that by the end of each month, you will have learned something extremely useful or have attained certain skills. Expect a coaching program based on the goals that you've set with your coach.

For the best results, I would endorse conducting at least one half hour coaching session per week. At the end of each coaching session, I give my client an assignment to be completed and submitted before the start of the next session.

CHAPTER 5

GETTING THE MOST

FROM BUSINESS COACHING

From the last chapter, you learned that most coaching programs will consist of 30-minute sessions held weekly or at least biweekly. Business coaching is a considerable investment, both in terms of time and money. It is, therefore, important that you get the most from each coaching session.

This chapter will detail how you can maximize the benefits business coaching brings by getting the most out of each session in order to improve yourself as an entrepreneur.

Determining whether your coach is right for you.

It is common in the practice of business coaching that the first coaching session be complimentary. This will allow you to determine whether this coach is right for you and for your coach to determine if you are a good fit for him or her. This session is a first date.

- Are you able to develop a rapport with this coach?
- Are you comfortable with his or her business experience?
- What type of people does he or she typically coach?
- Do you like his or her style of communication?
- What are some of his or her

accomplishments as a coach and business person?

- What industries does this coach have experience?

These are the five traits you should be looking for in a business coach:

1. Your coach has been successful with people in your particular industry or in working with other entrepreneurs to address similar business concerns.

2. Your coach has reached some career milestones. Great people are great teachers.

3. Your coach has gained success as well as failed a few times. This allows you to learn from their success as well as their mistakes.

4. You have some chemistry with your

coach. You don't have to be the best of friends, but should be able to hold interesting conversations with each other.

5.   Your coach should be passionate about making you more successful. A coach that spends a lot of time staring at the clock is only interested in their paycheck. They will do the bare minimum, and so you will see little improvement.

What to expect from your first session

Your first session should be quite relaxed. This is an opportunity to get to know your coach better and vice versa. Your business coach will be particularly interested in your current business situation. It is important that you don't hold back during your first session.

If your business or career is going through a

bad patch, let your coach know. Your goal should not be to impress your coach, but rather to impress upon them your current situation. The more they know about you, the better they can help you.

During your first session, any good coach will also want to know about your goals and how you plan to reach them. Your coach is also likely to ask about any actions you have taken to reach your goals. Be as open as possible about these things. Their job is to improve, motivate and inspire you to think big.

A good business coach will not just aimlessly direct you in achieving your goals. They will follow the SMARTd criteria:

Specific: They will mark a specific region to improve on.

Measurable: There should be a quantifiable way of measuring your progress.

Action Oriented: If there is anyone who will help you achieve your goals they must be identified. Your coach will help you in how to interact with such people for your benefit.

Realistic: Make sure your desired outcome is realistic. But at the same time make sure it is inspiring and somewhat out of your comfort zone; maybe even a smidge crazy. This will keep it interesting.

Time-bound: You need to give yourself a timeframe for when you hope to have achieved or made considerable progress towards reaching your goals.

detach - from the outcome. Just know that it

is already done. Own the identity that it is already who you are.

Do you remember when you were a child and your parent put a pot of water on the stove to boil? Did you ever sit and watch and wait for the water to boil? How long did it seem like it took? Perhaps it felt like forever? But it eventually boiled.

How do you do it now? I bet you turn on the stove, fill up a pot with water, put it on the flame and forget about it. And it boils every single time. Wow! You just have faith that it's going to boil because you know in your soul that it will. You don't need to keep checking on it. You just come back in a while, and you have a pot of boiling water.

Do this same thing with your outcomes; just set them up, and believe with absolute certainty that it will work out and detach from it. Let it go. Just know that it will work out. It truly is that simple.

Dos and don'ts during your coaching session

Due to the limited time you have during each coaching session, it is important that you follow certain rules in order to gain the most benefit.

- Do ask a lot of questions if you think it is relevant to the session.

- Do keep your responses as succinct as possible.

- Do learn to take criticism. Your business coach might point out a lot of flaws in your next business venture. They aren't trying to bring you down but to show you instead how to improve.

- Don't talk over your coach when they are

talking. You might miss a key point.

How to prepare for each coaching session

Business coaching is a highly developmental process. For this reason, as you reach new heights or experience lows in your business life, it is important that you keep your business coach informed. Before each session, there are a few things you need to bring with you. It is best to spend some time writing them down, so you don't forget.

- Make a note of how you spend time between each coaching session improving your business. It doesn't have to be actions such as "gained a new supplier". It could be something along the lines of "I learned how Facebook advertising could gain new customers."

Writing down new things that you have learned which will improve your business will help you remember to bring them up in your next session. There's nothing worse than leaving a meeting remembering afterward what it was you wanted to discuss in that session.

- Take a print out of a business article in your target industry that you found interesting and discuss it with your coach. The deeper you delve into your target industry, the higher the potential for your future success. Therefore, discussing current business events with your coach typically leads to thought-provoking discussions that spurn new ideas.

- Make a note about how you have spent time between each coaching session, making yourself a more efficient entrepreneur. Business is a highly competitive industry, and sometimes we allow setbacks to make us feel stressed and depressed. Chances are your coach has gone through the same experiences. For this reason, they can educate you on methods to reduce stress and handle pressure.

A man is a man because he is free to operate within his destiny. He is free to deliberate, to make decisions, and to choose between alternatives.

Martin Luther King Jr.

CHAPTER 6

AREAS WHERE A BUSINESS COACH CAN HELP

Business Planning

It's not too difficult to come up with a business plan these days. There are countless advice and many examples on blogs, consultant websites and business magazine websites throughout the internet.

A business coach is not necessarily there to help you write the technical aspects of your plan. After all, you most likely know more about your business than a business coach could know. However, a business coach will help with the most common question for most entrepreneurs, especially new entrepreneurs, when business planning; "Is this the right plan?"

We all know that entrepreneurial business endeavors are risky. But experienced entrepreneurs also know that reducing that risk through good planning and foresight is planning for success rather than taking a gamble. Successful entrepreneurs consider themselves risk takers, not gamblers.

A business coach will work with you to help you gain the confidence necessary to start that new business or move into a new direction with a current business. It is the business coach's role to help you see the things you already know and help you face the facts as necessary by providing an outside perspective.

So, how do you know that you have the right plan for your business?

To determine this, you should ask yourself a couple of questions.

1. Are you operating from your strengths, and

2. Are you coming from your place of passion?

The truth is you only have to be about 80% certain that you've made the right choice before you start moving. The other 20% will most likely take care of itself as you get started through minor adjustments along the way.

As in physics, it is much easier to change the course of an object once it has momentum. If you're not moving it means you won't have the ability to maneuver. You're just sitting on a fence.

So making a right commitment is like picking a runway when you're flying an airplane. Eventually, you're going to descend and make a landing. Before you take off, you have to choose the destination. The important part is that you liftoff. You get off the runway and on your way. Exactly how you get there may change from the initial plan along the way but you take off with the confidence that you will get there.

So pick an "airport," get off the ground and get some momentum. Along the way use your judgment to make course corrections and arrive at your destination in success. Don't seek 100% certainty. Get moving. Create motion. Gain momentum. That is what is going to work for you.

Failure

Are you great at failure? How do you manage your mindset during the ups and downs of your business? Well, you focus on what you do want, and not on what you don't want. Always accept, always know your outcome and know it with clarity.

How do you maintain confidence when experiencing failures in your business and life? Well, get used to making mistakes, they're a sign that you're making progress. And understand that failure is happening to serve you.

True failure only happens when you give up. Learn from other peoples' experience and their mistakes, that's how you develop judgment.

Model other peoples' success to apply that success to your life.

There is a formula for success and success builds upon success. Be good at failing. Fail fast, fail early. It's how you learn. That's how you get experience and eventually how you develop better judgment. It's a funny thing isn't it? Can you think of any time in your life when you learned something from being perfect? I can't.

Don't worry about failure; just use your experience to grow your business.

Time Management

For many entrepreneurs, there's never enough time in the day to get everything done. Interruptions, dealing with daily unexpected crises, distractions, phone calls, email and more can quickly turn a 12-hour workday into a loss.

Fortunately, that doesn't have to be the norm for you. A business coach can help you get into a proactive mindset, as opposed to reactive. Reactive busy work mode is where most people operate. They are just reacting to everything that's happening in their environment. In most cases, you might not even recognize specific time wasters.

If you're proactive, it means you know the outcome, and you're going for it and you're doing intelligent actions that get you towards it. You don't want to be doing urgent busy work.

It often feels like you're making progress when you're doing busy work. It's just like cleaning out your refrigerator. When you have something to do, it feels busy. It feels like you're making progress, but it's not going to get dollars in your bank account. What you want to do is things that are important and that matter. You want to be doing that most of the time.

One way to do this is to leverage other people by contracting out all of your busy work to other people who can do it much better than you. For example, get a housekeeper. Sure you might be able to clean your house, in just six hours, but what if you make 600 bucks an hour? You could pay a housekeeper 30 dollars an hour. They'll do a much better job and they'll do it in two hours. Isn't that the smart thing to do? So leverage your time and delegate as much as possible. That's how you manage your time as a business owner.

Life-Work Balance

How do you balance life and work? And as a business owner it often seems like you never have time for yourself. And that's true because having a business is similar to raising children. You must set boundaries, and you must have a balance in your life.

Most entrepreneurs neglect other parts of their life as their spouse, their friends or their health in pursuit of business success. Often not recognizing that neglecting these other areas of their life will eventually hinder their business success as well.

What you need to do is commit time to doing all things. You can't be everything all the time all at once. Since there are only 24 hours in each day, you have to divide it consciously. And a part of each day has to be dedicated to getting enough rest.

Set it up beforehand. Know what time you're going to start and stop work. Know what the projects are before you start. Know your outcomes before you start. Have situational and self-awareness about how you feel about each day before you start that day.

When you begin to feel tired, consciously make a decision to take a break. Enjoy your hobbies, spend time with your spouse, play with your children and get enough sleep each and every day. This will help you to remain creative and effective. If you're not effective, it's pointless to go on grinding. So that's how you're going to do it. You're going to set boundaries for yourself and that's going to create balance in your life.

Decision Making

As a business owner, making decisions is a daily if not hourly task. These decisions have an extraordinary impact on your business, your employees as well as you and your family. For most entrepreneurs, many of decisions are easily made throughout the course of the day. However, due to emotional attachments to their clients, services and products some decisions are very hard to recognize as a business's owner. Working with a business coach often provides the necessary impartial sounding board to help you see the need for certain decisions in your business as well as helping you come to a decision.

As a commercial pilot, I was trained to make decisions using the DECIDE model. DECIDE is an aviation acronym.

Detect that a change has occurred and that you need to change something to address it.

Estimate the necessary change to get back to where you want to be.

Choose an outcome. Where do you want to end up?

Identify your options to get to where you want to go.

Do one of the options.

Evaluate how it worked and continue to do this process.

Another part of decision-making that's really

important is using your intuition. We're all raised to think that there are five senses; vision, auditory, kinesthetic, taste, smell. There is also a sixth sense.

The sixth sense is intuition. And that is something that's infinitely powerful, and it comes with incredible accuracy. You are always right when you think with your heart. A challenge is learning how to interpret your intuition and pay attention to it.

So ultimately intelligent decision-making has two parts. You have to use your head and your heart. The head is the DECIDE model. Your heart is your intuition. When you combine both, you can make effective decisions that work in your business.

Creating a Team Environment

Successful entrepreneurs aren't typically lone wolves. Their business success often depends on other people, such as employees, an executive team, advisory board and independent contractors. Therefore, creating and maintaining a team environment in a business is a chief ongoing concern for most entrepreneurial leaders.

A business coach can help you not only create that team environment but also help you continuously generate new ideas on how to maintain it and keep it fresh.

Let's talk about the E-Myth concept. E-Myth stands for entrepreneurial myth; a concept author Michael Gerber discusses in his book "The E-Myth Revisited." In the book, Michael states that there are three distinct personalities in business. Old school thinking states that business people could be a jack of all trades; that they could possess all three personalities and be effective and successful. If you try to do that now, you're going to get smoked.

Michael's E-Myth concept makes the case that in order to be effective and successful in business you must pick your strength. You must come to a realization of what your strength is, develop it and use it to mastery. Those areas where you are not as strong should be delegated to others that are strong in those areas.

These three personality/skill areas are:

Artist/Technician

These are people that are very accomplished in a specific skill or knowledge base. It could be that they have a specialized skill set or are naturally gifted in an area of their business or career.

Entrepreneur

These are people that are not only creators but also enjoy taking risks. Entrepreneurs, as described by Gerber, are willing to chance losing it all for the opportunity to make substantial gains.

Leader Manager

Leader/Managers are people persons. They are skilled at working with people and truly love working with others and get a charge out of inspiring people.

A business coach can help you determine which one of these categories is your true strength. Determine this and then find and work with other people that have primary strengths in the other areas to create a dynamic team.

When creating a team environment, there are four phases that every team goes through.

1. **Forming Phase** - That's where the team is coming together, everyone is inspired, and things are looking great.

2. **Storming Phase** - During this phase, people start to disagree, and it gets hard. The truth is commitment starts when the fun stops. Sometimes people don't want to hear that. If they think it's not fun, they give up, or they say, "I'm going to try something that's easier." The truth is, every team goes through the storm phase.

3. **Norming Phase** - Norming is when operations start to become normal. The storm subsides, and people begin to get

into a groove. During this phase, you will start to see results.

4. **Performing Phase**. - The final stage represents team maturity. The team is performing like a well-oiled machine. This is where everyone wants to be when they envision a team environment. The reality is that you must go through the previous three phases to get here.

When creating a team, first recognize that you can't do it all yourself. Determine your strengths and find people with strengths that compliment you. Accept the four phases of team building and push through the storm to get to the perform.

Recognizing Successes

At first, learning how to recognize success might seem silly. After all, we all have some gut level vision of what success means to each of us. However, ask most people to define that vision of success on paper and they'll likely get stuck.

The fact is we all have successes every day and might not even recognize them as such without the insight of someone outside ourselves. Most of us are so busy moving from one problem to another that we don't take the time to look back on our successes and whether or not those successes are getting us where when want to go.

As a business coach, I help entrepreneurs not only define success for themselves but also help them recognize the not so obvious successes that occur along the way to achieving their ultimate goal. Here's how I help my clients measure success.

Success is when you arrive at your smart outcome. By determining what success is before you start the journey you can recognize when you have finally arrived at your destination. SMARTd is another acronym.

S – Specific
You must know exactly where you're going. Just like a pilot filing a flight plan you need to be specific about your destination.

M – Measurable
Your desired outcome must be measurable to enable you to make course adjustments along the way. This is where a coach can be very helpful.

A - Action Oriented

Your desired outcome must be based around a series of actions that you can take to move forward.

R – Realistic

Make sure your desired outcome is realistic. But at the same time make sure it is inspiring and somewhat out of your comfort zone; maybe even a smidge crazy. This will keep it interesting.

T – Time

In order to achieve something you must give yourself a deadline otherwise, you're just going to keep extending the time frame and that's just not the way it works.

d – Detach

Detach from the outcome. Just know that it is already done. Own the identity that it is already who you are. Set up for your outcomes, and believe with absolute certainty that it will work out and detach from it. Let it go. Just know that it will work out. It truly is that simple.

So SMART people always have SMARTd outcomes and are readily able to recognize their success.

Mission Statement

How do you create a mission statement for your business? Well, start with your identity. Who are you? What's your purpose? Make it simple.

You know, probably the best mission statement I ever came across was for a business where I used to work. Have you heard of those restaurants called Dukes? It's a company called TS Restaurants. Their mission statement is three parts:

"Have fun, Make money, with Aloha."

Everyone that worked there loved it. We lived it and it was easy. We all had fun at work. We made money while working with aloha. Simple is good, so make it simple. You also have to understand which problems you are attempting to solve and which solutions you are attempting to put into place. You also have to consider what the pain you are trying to avoid is and what is the pleasure that you're trying to achieve. Those are the most important things you need to consider when creating a mission statement. When you do that, it's easy.

> What is success? I think it's a mixture of having a flair for thing that you are doing; knowing that it is not enough, that you have got to have hard work and a certain sense of purpose.
>
> Margaret Thatcher

CHAPTER 7

WHAT TO LOOK FOR IN A BUSINESS COACH

It is true that some business coaches are much better fits for you than others. Since you will most likely find a business coach through a referral or online it's always good practice to get a good feel for someone before leaping into a new relationship. Take some extra time to fully know a prospective coach. Below are ten qualities you ought to look for in a business coach:

Experience

The very first thing to look at in a business coach's resume is their experience. What have they exactly accomplished, better yet what have they helped others accomplish, and is that what you desire to accomplish? The coach you are looking for should have walked in your footsteps and helped others do the same. Get someone who can talk about real-life occurrences, where they have succeeded and where they have failed. This will build your confidence that you are working with someone with whom you can build a report; raising your opportunity of immense success.

Clarity about the Entire Process

Skilled and good business coaches are able to walk an entrepreneur through their business process. This process includes helping an entrepreneur define their core challenges, and gaining a clear understanding of where they are now to where they want to go. It is also important that the coach describes how to learn new abilities and behaviors. You should also look for a coach that is willing to chip in and help you transfer those ideas back to your team.

Accessibility

A reliable business coach must always be reachable. He or she must be willing to create a program specific to you as a client since one size never fits all. Determine whether you both share common values and concerns. You're looking for a coach that is looking to win with you. You can also discuss their schedules and see where you fit in.

A Good Business Coach Should Have Expectations of You

A good and reliable coach will always hold you accountable. They must be able to outline what they require from you, action and time wise. If your coach doesn't ask you what your capabilities are, that's a red flag. This is because a coach needs to know what you can or cannot do so that they may know how to help you or provide constructive feedback about your skills.

Able to Draw Out Your Best Thinking

When it comes to business, your best assets are your brain and your gut instinct. It's, therefore, essential to look for a coach who can listen sincerely and facilitate your very best thinking. They should not just jump directly to conclusions without assisting you first to organize your own thoughts. Innovation will result from your two skill sets, hence find someone who will compliment and advise you, not overpower you.

Connections

A great business coach will be willing to connect you with people who can benefit you, in the long run. He or she may have connections with greater and new business opportunities, which they think can assist you in your line of business. You can ask them if they are willing to help open new doors.

Confidentiality

A good and reliable business coach should be willing to defend your well-being through discretion and should never share any information concerning you to anyone. Good business coaches make clear agreements on discretion upfront with their clients. If the agreement is broken, it will be good to end the relationship as this could greatly damage your line of business.

Willing To Share

Look for a coach who is willing to share all of their experiences; the bad and the good. They should be able to admit their failures freely as they learned from their past errors. If you get the feeling that they are holding back, it surely is not a good sign. You will learn more with somebody who is radically transparent.

A Love for Coaching

Good coaches love to coach other people and offer assistance where needed. How a prospective coach treats you from the start of your encounter is the best indicator of how they will act in due course. Check how they get to your first appointment or how delicate they take your issues to be. You surely require a coach who is thoughtful of your time and money.

Great Support

Last but not least, a great business coach is always supportive. They are there to support you even if there is no one else who believes in you or supports your vision. He or she should be there to define your objectives and break them down in little steps so you can see success along your way. They should be able to motivate you in every way possible.

A Servant's Heart

When speaking with various people it's common to feel like you are being sold. We often get this feeling when we are interacting with a person who is manipulating us. It feels very transactional; like they are trying to take your resources through high-pressure sales tactics. There are so many salesey people and techniques out there. I think that I can speak for just about everyone and say that it doesn't work. It's an instant turn-off and not a sustainable way to do business.

I believe in an even value exchange, or

perhaps giving way more than is expected. The best coaches are servants of their clients. We are deeply committed to serving you, and not just making a transaction. You get a feeling in your heart when someone is serving you. You can feel it. Their needs are your needs too.

Much of the time it may feel good, and yet a coach who is truly committed to service is willing to take you out of your comfort zone and risk getting fired to help you achieve success with your results. A true servant coach is not there to affirm you but to tell you the truth under the umbrella of rapport. I am willing to communicate my perspective with you and even break rapport at times.

You don't have to "like" me all of the time; that's not realistic. In fact, there may be moments when you feel like quitting. An outstanding coach will take you to this point and challenge you to stretch yourself further, past your perceived limits and help you to own that extra increment of your performance that you weren't aware that you even possess. And the truth is that this place is out of your comfort zone.

In fact; EVERYTHING YOU WANT IS OUT OF YOUR COMFORT ZONE. The only way to get what you want is to get out of your comfort zone, and a coach with a servant's heart will help you get what you really want and need. We can help you to own your results in your mind before they have come to fruition in the real world. An outstanding coach is your servant in many ways.

> It doesn't matter which side of the fence you get off on sometimes. What matters most is getting off. You cannot make progress without making decisions.
>
> Jim Rohn

CHAPTER 8

WHAT YOU SHOULD DO NEXT

I'm looking for a "dream" client. An entrepreneur that I can help get massive results.

If you are that client, I'd like to work with you side-by-side to help you break through to the next level of your business and career, increasing revenue and overall life satisfaction over the next 12 months.

The first thing we will do is meet for a

discovery session where we will work on determining some of your short term goals and creating a strategic plan to achieve those goals and get you immediate results. This meeting will only take about 30 to 45 minutes and is held online or by telephone.

You pay nothing for this meeting and strategic coaching plan. It's my way of helping you determine whether or not I would be a good coach for you. While at the same time, it gives me a chance to determine how I can be of help to you in your business and life.

At the end of this session, one of two things will happen.

One – You love the plan, gained insight on how you should proceed and decide to take it on your own.

If that's the case, I'll wish you the best of luck and ask you to keep me posted on your progress.

OR

Two – You love the plan, gain insight, feel you'll benefit from my coaching style, we both experience a chemistry between us that you just know will breed continued success and you ask to become my client so we can work together and implement the plan.

When that happens, together we'll explode your mindset and reveal opportunities to increase your wealth, health and happiness in your business and life.

It is that simple. There is no catch.

The worst that can happen is you get an

opportunity to experience a coaching session with me free and walk away with some insights that you can act on immediately.

On the other hand, I jump in your Co-Pilot seat and we work together one-on-one to blow away your limiting beliefs, chart a navigational course for the next successful chapter in your business and do what it takes to make it happen this year.

Just shoot me an email at dru@powercurvecoaching.com (my personal address) and we can get started.

BONUS

Free DiSC Index Assessment

As a bonus to purchasing this book, I'm offering you a **free DiSC Index** personal assessment (easily a $100+ value). This DiSC Index Assessment will provide you with an understanding of your personality and communication style, as well as help you identify  the best way to communicate with the people you lead.

You can get this bonus by visiting http://www.PowerCurveCoaching.com/disc and following the instructions there. Offer is good while supplies last.

Power Curve Coaching

www.PowerCurveCoaching.com

Business Coaching Videos

Dru Eats the Dog Food!

That's right, Dru eats a can of Trader Joe's Chunky dog food in this video. As a challenge to meet his goal with a client, Dru steps up. Visit the link below to see this incredibly funny moment and gain access to several of Dru's business coaching videos.

www.PowerCurveCoaching.com/videos

and many more …

ABOUT THE AUTHOR

Dru Babcock is a Mentor at Founders Space and a Peak-performance Coach/Author with Power Curve Coaching. He will assist you in designing and creating your company into fruition while thriving in an exponentially changing technology environment. He is a Certified Flight Instructor and former Commercial Pilot.

Dru has worked with over one thousand individuals, companies and groups in the past 20 years in successfully achieving their business, flight, athletic, relationship and life results. He is an active entrepreneur and specializes in assisting people who own and operate local and global companies. He has earned his position as a member of the premier team of world-class coaches, who are known as the "Seal Team Six" of the coaching industry, founded by an industry father. With his deep understanding of psychology and strategy, he can coach you and your team to success with your business and life results.

He graduated the University of San Francisco, McLaren School of Business and has deep roots in San Francisco. He is a lifelong amateur athlete in the areas of Kite-boarding, sailing, skiing, surfing and fitness/adventure Challenges. Dru is here to serve you in going from where you are to where you want to be; in the least amount of time and steps while passionately enjoying the incredible journey of being an entrepreneur!